Reef and Freshwater Fish of Seychelles
a field guide

Oliver, Justin and Robin Gerlach

Text by Oliver Gerlach

Illustrations by Justin Gerlach

Design by Robin Gerlach

1st edition 2007
2nd edition 2014, Phelsuma Press
http://islandbiodviersity.com/Phelsumapress.htm

CONTENTS

Introduction	3
Sharks, Remora and Guitarfish	6
Rays	8
Eels and eel-like fish	10
Mullet, barracuda, milkfish, bonefish, terapon, monocle bream, fuisiliers	12
Trumpetfish, cornetfish, pipefish, shrimpfish	14
Coralfish	16
Scorpionfish	18
Sweetlips, batfish, moony	20
Gobies, blennies, sand smelt, lizardfish	22
Spinefoots, flying fish, halfbeaks, sweepers, goldies, cardinalfish, goatfish	24
Angelfish	26
Soldierfish, squirrelfish, bullseye	28
Wrasse	30
Tang	32
Parrotfish	35
Triggerfish, filefish	37
Puffers, cowfish, boxfish, porcupinefish	39
Snappers and emperors	41
Gamefish	43
Jack, tuna	45
Damselfish	47
Groupers	50
Estuarine and freshwater fish	52

INTRODUCTION

This guide aims to provide easy identification of the fish found on and around all the islands within the Republic of Seychelles. It is a companion guide to the "Vertebrates of Seychelles" guide. Previously much of the marine fauna has been difficult to identify owing to the fact that all literature on the subject refers to a wider geographical area except the main reference to Seychelles fish, Smith and Smith's "Fishes of Seychelles" is difficult to obtain and to use. This book covers the species most likely to be seen, that is, the most common or conspicuous marine and estuarine fish. These include reef fish, gamefish, food fish and estuarine/freshwater fish. The first attempt at a comprehensive listing of Seychelles fish (1969) recorded 775 species, and another 100 were added in 1992. The current total is 1192 species, but more are regularly discovered.

Short accounts of the commonest and most distinctive species are given here. Typical colour forms are illustrated; in species with distinctive sexual dimorphism or distinctive juveniles these are also illustrated.

Coral bleaching

In 1998 there was extensive coral bleaching caused by constant raised water temperatures. The damage was unprecedented, with some reefs showing 95% coral mortality. The high temperatures caused the corals to eject the beneficial algae on which they depended for food during the day. Without this extra food, the polyps starved and died. When the coral died, algae started growing, leading to large areas of reef changing from the multi-coloured living coral reef to white coral skeletons and patches of green algae.

The bleaching affected other organisms, including sea anemones that also used symbiotic algae and the organisms that depended upon corals and anemones. Most reef fish were not affected by the initial bleaching although impacts on some species were significant. Those that were badly affected include specialised coral feeders such as harlequin filefish and shrimpfish. These disappeared in 1998 and are only now starting to reappear in some areas, some 10 years later. Other species benefited from the increased algal growth on the dead coral. These were the grazers such as parrotfish, rabbitfish and tangs. Enormous shoals of which can be seen on many damaged reefs. Interestingly, it has been discovered that the grazers are chased away from the territories of territorial damselfish, thus creating a patchy weedbed. In the absence of grazers, sea urchins build up to eat the algae. The sea urchins also eroding the substrate and large populations of these wear down the coral, inhibiting new growth. The late 20th century was a time of great change in the Indo-Pacific coral reefs and this continues. Whether natural coral reefs will be able to recover in the long-term remains to be seen.

Areas of special interest

Almost all coastal areas of Seychelles support interesting marine habitats and isolated coral heads with dramatic fish populations can be found in virtually every bay. Areas of special interest for marine fauna are the marine national parks of:

Curieuse – Curieuse bay supports a wide range of habitats, there are no extensive reefs but patch reefs have very good coral regrowth in some areas. Particularly interesting are the granite rocks around Curieuse.

Ste Anne – this was the first marine national park to be established in Seychelles. For many years its convenient location and outstanding fringing reefs made it one of the most important tourist attractions in the islands. The coastal reclamation along the east coast of Mahé from 1986 to the present has led to large amounts of silt entering the park. This, combined with pollution from Port Victoria, means that most of the coral reef is now dead and covered by a film of silt and algae.

Cap Ternay – this area appears to have been partially sheltered from the raised temperatures causing the coral bleaching event of 1998. The coral reef is in comparatively good condition although not extensive.

Silhouette – Silhouette is the least well known of the marine national parks. It has some fringing reef but is outstanding for granite boulder formations and caves. There are isolated areas with some coral regrowth. A good location for turtles as well as a wide variety of fish.

Cocos – is visited by large numbers of snorkellers and can be overcrowded at times. The coral habitats are interesting although the fantastic groves of stagshorn that used to occur in shallow water and now all dead.

Aride – Aride has poor snorkelling due to a very localised reef and strong currents although it provides dramatic and interesting diving conditions.

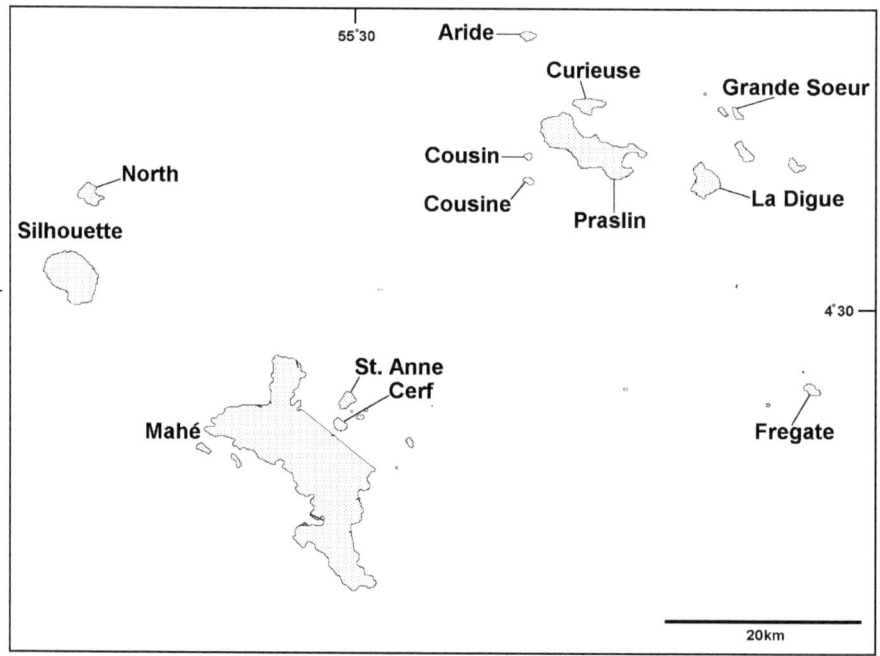

Granitic islands of Seychelles

Other good areas are the islands of:

Praslin – localised areas are good for snorkelling, especially among the rocks at Anse Lazio, good diving is more extensive.

Mahé – although heavily developed and with widespread pollution problems there are a number of good diving sites. Snorkelling is easily undertaken from many places but is of relatively poor quality.

Shark bank – a deep water bank, notable mostly for its large predatory fish. Suitable only for diving.

La Digue – good diving especially between La Digue and nearby islands, generally not notable for snorkelling.

Desroches – before coral bleaching Desroches provided some of the most accessible and best coral for snorkelling, this is now mainly dead, although with some areas of regrowth. Diving is good in deeper water, with a dramatic 'drop-off'.

Alphonse – Alphonse and the St. Francois atoll provide excellent diving in deep water around the atoll rim. Snorkelling is not easy and not outstanding.

Astove – a short way beyond the small reef flat on the west side of the island there are a large number of interesting cliffs on the 'drop-off' to 2000 m.

Cosmoledo - Cosmoledo has extremely good coral regrowth. Several species of large sponge have been found, as have huge numbers of potato cod.

Aldabra – Aldabra has outstanding diving, with a healthy reef and large numbers of large fish and marine invertebrates that have become rare elsewhere. Snorkelling is generally difficult but drift-snorkelling on the inflowing current into the lagoon is a remarkable experience.

SHARKS (Plate 1)
33 species of shark have been recorded in Seychelles. Only the species covered below can be regarded as commonly seen, although others may be numerous in some areas. Although famed as marine predators and widely feared shark attacks are extremely rare and none have been reported in Seychelles.

Whale shark *Rhincodon typus* (1)
The whale shark is the largest living species of fish, growing up to 20 m long and weighing up to 34,000 kg. It is a filter-feeding surface dweller that is found in open water. The skin of this massive shark can be up to 10 cm thick. This species is also a livebearer, but the number of pups produced is unknown. The Whale Shark swims by moving its whole body from side to side, unlike other sharks, which swim by moving only the tail. The method used by the Whale Shark is not very fast, so its maximum speed is 5 kph. It is a solitary shark, and groups are very rare, but may form in good feeding areas, especially off the coast of Mahé.

Whitetip reef shark *Triaenodon obesus* (3)
This species is mainly nocturnal, and so adults usually spend most of the day in deep caves and crevices in the coral while the juveniles come into the shallows to feed on worms in the sand. It can commonly be found on reefs, but sometimes in open water. It feeds on coral fishes and crustaceans, and only rarely comes near the surface. The average size for a whitetip reef shark is about 140-160 cm, but they do get up to 210. It is a livebearer, and females enter shallow bays to give birth to 1-5 pups, usually 2-3, that are 50-60 cm long at birth. This species lives up to about 25 years old.

Nurse shark *Nebrius concolor* (4)
The depth range of the nurse shark is from 1 to 70 m. It is a bottom-dwelling shark that can be found on the outer edges of reefs and lagoons. It is mainly nocturnal, but is sometimes seen in caves in coral and on flat sand, singly or in piles of several individuals. It feeds on benthic invertebrates, fish, cephalopods, echinoderms and crustaceans. There are four or more pups in a litter. It uses its large pharynx as a suction pump to inhale small creatures that are out of range of its teeth. They may also reverse this action to blast streams of water at predators.

REMORA (Plate 1)
Remora *Echineis naucrates* (2)
The remora is a strange fish that grows to about 110 cm long. It attaches itself to sharks, rays big fishes, turtles, whales, and sometimes ships by the sucker on the back of its head. It eats detritus and zooplankton. Juveniles occasionally act as parrotfish cleaners. Sometimes the remora is used as an aid to fishing. A line is tied to the tail, and then the remora is released. It fastens itself to a fish, and then remora and host are pulled up. Three species of remora occur in Seychelles.

Plate 1

GUITAR FISH (Plate 1)
Giant guitar fish *Rhynchobatus djiddensis* (5)
The guitar fish are a very primitive family of cartilaginous fish, in Seychelles three

species have been recorded. They are very similar to the rays in that they have large extended pectoral fin that look like wings. The giant guitar fish grows up to 3 m long and can weigh up to 227 kg. It is a bottom dweller and can be found in muddy and sandy substrates in estuaries, lagoons, and near to reefs. It eats clams, crustaceans and small fish. There are usually between 4 and 10 pups in a litter.

RAYS (Plate 2)
11 species of ray have been recorded in Seychelles, the three commonest and the largest species are described below.

Giant manta *Manta birostris* (1)
The "wingspan" of the manta is up to 7 m, and it can weigh as much as 1,400 g. It can commonly be found in open water near the shore, at mid-depth. The Manta is a solitary species of ray, but when there is a high concentration of food in an area, large numbers may be seen. They may leap out of the water, landing with a loud, distinctive slap. It eats plankton, and the paddle-like projections on either side of the mouth are for channelling food. When not feeding, the ray folds the projections back against it mouth. There are about 2 pups in a litter, and there is often 2 year gap between litters. They were formerly common in the granitic islands but now are rarely seen except in the Amirantes and southern atolls.

Spotted eagle ray *Aetobatus narinari* (2)
The spotted eagle ray has a "wingspan" of up to 3 m, and can weigh up to about 230 kg. It can be found in coastal waters, in bays and on reefs, at depths down to 80 m. These rays are commonly seen as solitary individuals or in large groups. When seen in groups they are always near the surface, and will sometimes leap out of the water. There are about 4 live young in a litter. The mouth has been specially adapted for crushing shellfish, and has single row of teeth, flattened into a large smooth plate on each jaw.

Torpedo ray *Torpedo fuscomatulata* (3)
The Torpedo ray is a bottom dwelling species of electric ray. It can produce up to 37 volts of electricity which it uses to stun its prey. The maximum size of a torpedo ray is 64 cm. It eats cephalopods and small fish.

Blotched fantail ray *Taeninura melanospilos* (4)
The blotched fantail ray has a maximum length of 3 m with tail, and a "wingspan" of up to 180cm. It can weigh up to 150 kg. It eats small bottom dwelling fish and crustaceans. The mouth is positioned on the underside of the body so that the ray can scoop up small creatures hiding in the sand. There are up to 7 pups in a litter.

Plate 2

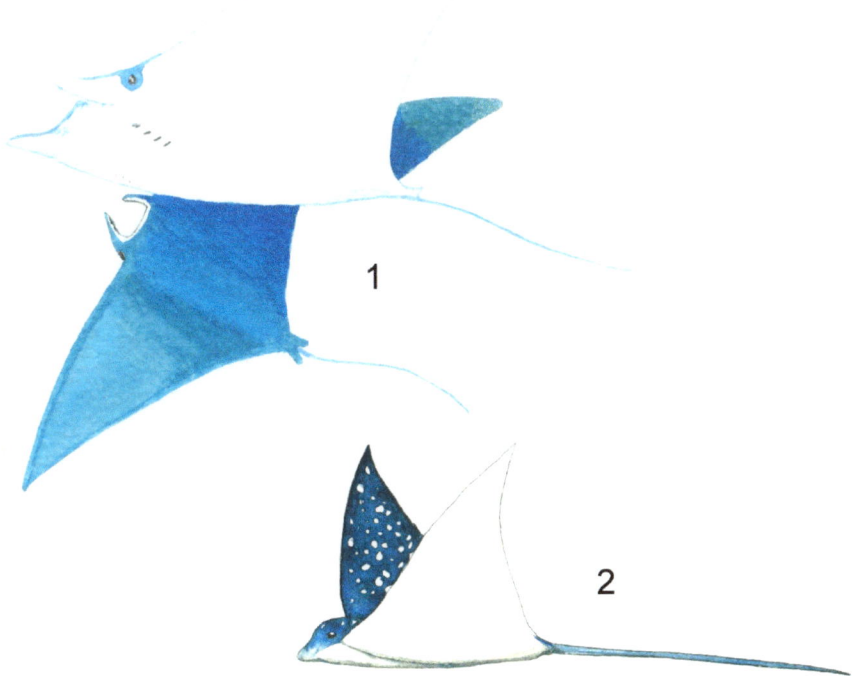
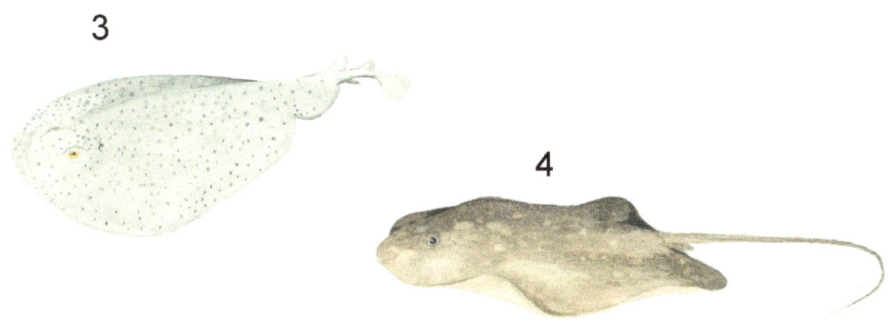

EELS AND EEL-LIKE FISH (Plate 3)

Barbel eel *Plotosus lineatus* (6)
The barbel eel can grow as big as 32 cm long and as old as 7 years. They can be found in huge shoals over sandy areas. They are found at depths of up to 80 m. Although juveniles are usually seen in dense ball-like shoals in the shallow water of lagoons. The fin spines are extremely venomous. They eat worms, molluscs, fish and cephalopods.

EELS

There are 50 eel species in Seychelles of several different families, the most diverse family is the morays with 31 species. There is only species of **conger eel** found in Seychelles; *Conger cinereus* (2) grows up to at least 130cm long and has been seen 80m below the surface. Below the surface. It hunts for fish and crustaceans at night, assuming a pattern of broad dark grey vertical stripes. This species is common in eelgrass beds and reef flats. It is also occasionally seen in estuaries. There are many species of moray eel, but the 4 most common are:

starry moray *Echidna nebulosa* (3)
zebra moray *Gymnomuraena zebra* (4)
yellow-edged moray *Gymnothorax flavimarginatus* (5) and
white moray *Siderea grisea* (1)

The largest known size for a moray is 150 cm. They have a depth range of 1-50 m. Juveniles are found in eelgrass beds and sandy areas, and adults hide under the rocks on reef flats and in caves in the reef. They eat crustaceans and fish, and *Gymnothorax* will also eat molluscs and sea urchins.

Plate 3

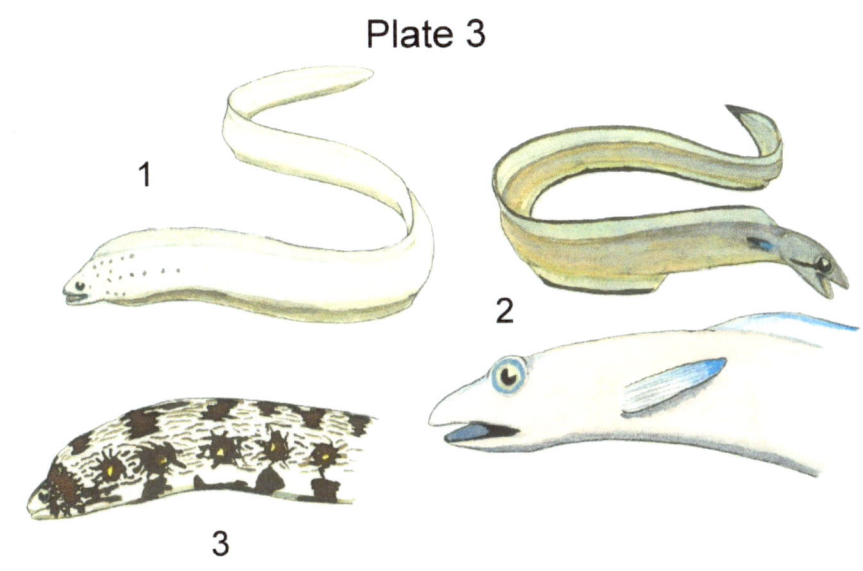

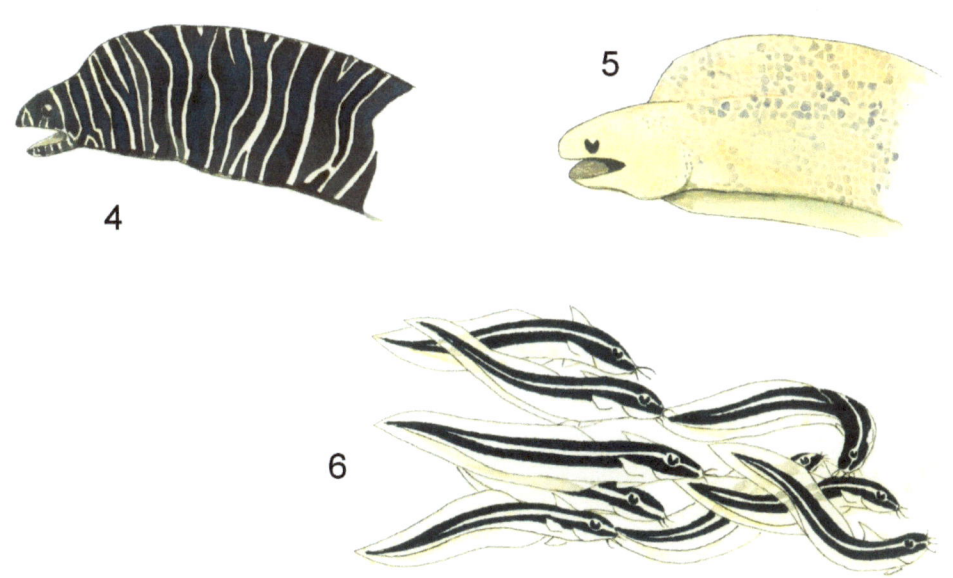

MULLET (Plate 4)
The ten species of mullet found in Seychelles include the **fringe-lip mullet** *Crenimugil crenilabis* (1). They can grow up to 60 cm long and can be as old as 14 years. Their depth range is from the surface to 20 m they are found in shoals in coastal waters over sandy or muddy areas of estuaries, lagoons and reef flats. They eat detritus containing algae and microscopic animals by scooping up the top layer of sand or mud and filtering it through their gills.

BARRACUDA (Plate 4)
Barracuda have a depth range of 0-200m. They are solitary, but juveniles shoal. They eat fish, but will sometimes take squid. Barracuda are food fish. They are commonly seen in shallow water near the coast. There are 8 species found in Seychelles, of which the **giant barracuda** *Sphyraenea barracuda* is the largest and the **pickhandle barracuda** *S. jello* (2) one of the most abundant. This latter species is typical of most barracudas. Of these, the only species known to attack humans is *Barracuda*. Attacks have not happened in Seychelles, but do happen rarely in the Pacific Ocean; when they happen, one quick strike is enough to leave a person severely wounded. Fatalities are very rare.

MILKFISH AND BONEFISH (Plate 4)
Bonefish *Albula vulpes* (3)
The bonefish is very similar to the milkfish in many ways, but the bonefish is the smaller of the two, only growing up to 140 cm long and weighing up to 10 kg. It can be found in shoals over shallow sandy areas. It eats worms, crustaceans, molluscs and cephalopods. This species is too bony to be edible, but fly fishing for sporting purposes is popular and important in the St. Francois atoll near Alphonse.

Milkfish *Chanos chanos* (4)
Male milkfish can grow up to 180 cm. long, and females up to 124 cm. They can weigh as much as 140 kg. The maximum recorded age for a milkfish is 15 years. It is a coastal shoaling fish that will often enter estuaries and streams. They eat algae, plankton and fish eggs. The fry eat plankton.

TERAPON (Plate 4)
Jaruba terapon *Terapon jarbua* (6)
The maximum size for a terapon is 35cm. The adults have a depth range of 20-290 m, but juveniles are always seen in shallow lagoons (0-2 m depth). They are found in schools of 3-10 fish. They eat small fish, insects and sand dwelling invertebrates.

MONOCLE BREAM (Plate 4)
Bridled monocle bream *Scolopsis frenatus* (5)
Monocle breams can grow up to 25 cm long and are found singly near the bottom over

Plate 4

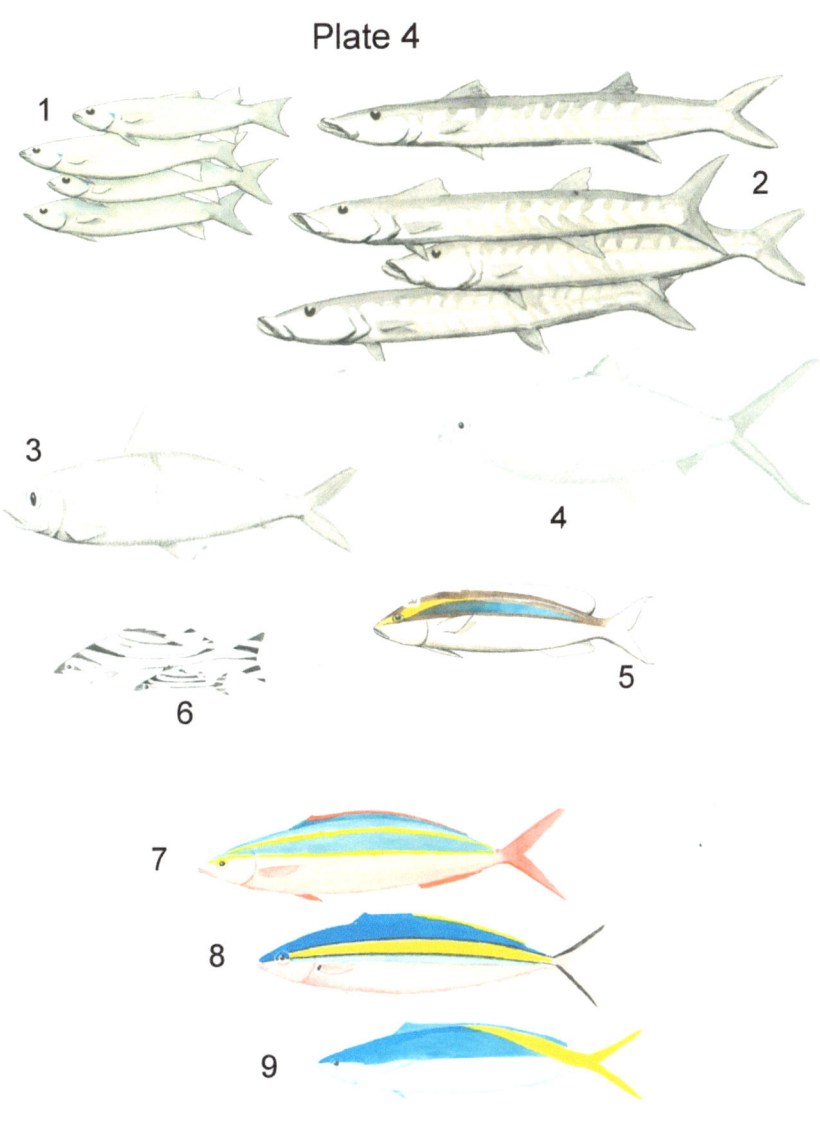

sandy areas and reefs at depths of 5-20 m. They eat plankton.

FUSILIERS (Plate 4)

Fusiliers can be found in shoals near coral reefs in deep lagoons. Juveniles are occasionally used as tuna bait. The common size for a fusilier is between 30 and 40 cm long. They are found in depths of 5-50m. below the surface. They are 6 species of

Pterocaesio and 5 of *Caesio* found in Seychelles. They change colour to a dull red or blue at night. Common species include
Two-lined fusilier *Pterocaesio diagramma* (7)
Blue and yellow fusilier *Caesio caerulaea* (8)
Yellowback fusilier *C. teres* (9)

TRUMPETFISH AND CORNETFISH (Plate 5)
Chinese trumpetfish *Aulostomus chinensis* (1)
Trumpetfish can be found at depths of up to 120 m. It can grow up to 80 cm long. It eats small fish and shrimps. It is a slow swimming solitary fish that hunts by coming up behind its prey and attacking. It is usually found at the edges of reefs and in seagrass beds. It occasionally "rides" behind larger fish in order to ambush prey.

Red cornetfish *Fistularia petimba* (2)
Two very similar cornetfish or flutemouth species have been recorded in Seychelles. The depth range of the red cornetfish is 2-200 m. They can grow up to 2 m long and the heaviest recorded is 4.5 kg. They eat fish and shrimps. They usually swim slowly and may appear motionless.

PIPEFISH (Plate 5)
20 species of pipefish and seahorses have been recorded in Seychelles. These are very rarely seen with the exception of the network pipefish. There are very few records of seahorses. In addition to the one common pipefish species the strange and easily overlooked ghost pipefish is illustrated.

Network pipefish *Corythoicthys flavofasciatus* (3)
The network pipefish grows up to 12 cm long and can occasionally be found in seagrass beds, but most often in algae-matted rock and coral up to a depth of 25 m below the surface. The male carries the eggs after they have been laid. This is the most common pipefish in Seychelles.

Ghost pipefish *Solenostomus cyanopterus* (4)
The ghost pipefish is an uncommon species that grows up to 17 cm long. It is found in coastal areas and weedbeds at depths of up to 25 m but usually near the surface. It is a monogamous species, and is always seen in pairs. They breed hidden in seaweed. They eat small crustaceans and fish fry.

SHRIMPFISH (Plate 5)
Shrimpfish *Aeoliscus strigatus* (5)
Shrimpfish grow up to 15 cm long and are found at depths of 1-20 m. They are always seen in small synchronized shoals, nose down in *Diadema* urchins or stagshorn corals. They eat microscopic crustaceans.

Plate 5

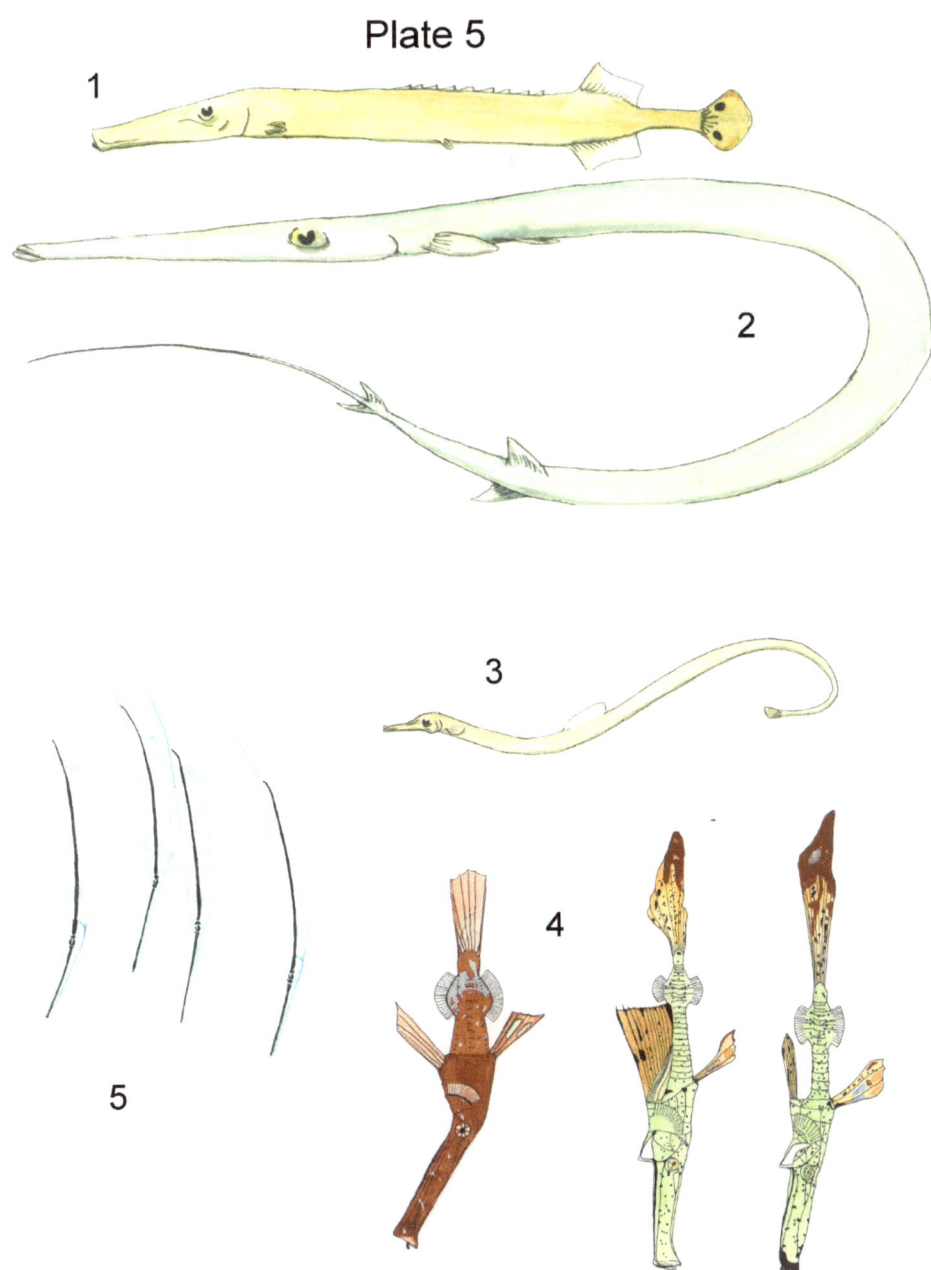

CORALFISH AND OTHERS (Plate 6)

Coralfish are one of the most distinctive fish families on coral reefs. 30 species have been recorded in Seychelles, 8 of the most common species are illustrated here along with the coachman and the Moorish idol which occur in similar habitats.

Scrawled butterflyfish *Chaetodon meyeri* (1)
Scrawled butterflyfish are found in coral heads at depths of up to 25 m. They feed exclusively on coral polyps, and so they were depreciated in numbers by the coral bleaching. Juveniles are seen singly, and adults are found in pairs.

Zanzibar butterflyfish *Chaetodon zanzibarensis* (2)
The maximum size for a Zanzibar butterflyfish is 12 cm. They are found singly or in small groups in the branches of *acropora* corals at depths of 3-40 m. They eat coral polyps.

Longnose butterflyfish *Forcipier longirostris* (3)
This is an uncommon species of butterflyfish that is found on reefs at depths of up to 60 m. This is a specialised feeder on small invertebrates in crevices in the coral reef.

Melon butterflyfish *Chaetodon trifasciatus* (4)
Melon butterflyfish can grow up to 15cm. long and have a depth range of 2-20m. they are found in coral-rich lagoons and reefs. they are territorial fish and are highly aggressive towards other butterflyfish. They are seen in pairs. juveniles hide in corals. They exclusively the polyps of *pocillopora* corals.

Threadfin butterflyfish *Chaetodon auriga* (5)
Threadfin butterflyfish are found in reefs and weedy or rubbly areas. They are seen singly, in pairs and in small groups. They feed by tearing bits off worms, anemones, coral polyps and algae.

Racoon butterflyfish *Chaetodon lunula* (6)
Racoon butterflyfish can grow up to 20 cm long and are seen in lagoons and reefs at depths of up to 30 m. They eat tubeworm tentacles, nudibranchs, other benthic invertebrates, algae and coral polyps.

Vagabond butterflyfish *Chaetodon vagabundus* (7)
These can grow to 23 cm. They are found in reef flats and lagoons, somtimes down to 20 m. They eat algae, coral polyps, crustaceans and worms. They are seen in pairs.

Moorish idol *Zanclus cornutus* (8)
Moorish idols can grow up to 23 cm long and are found in reefs and lagoons at depths of 2-180 m. They are usually seen in groups of 2 or 3, and very rarely in large shoals. They eat small animals encrusted onto rocks.

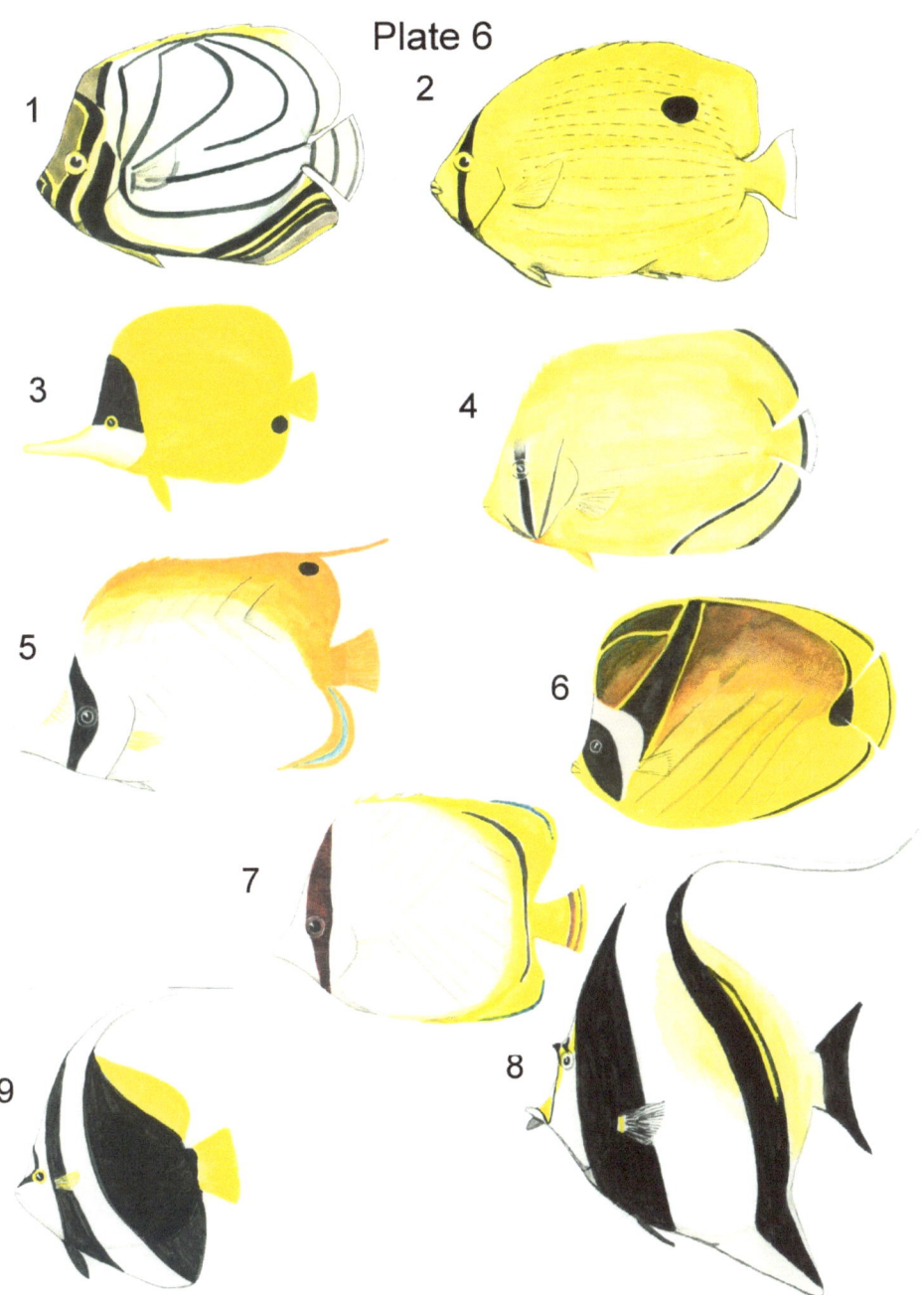

Coachman *Heniochus monoceros* (9)
Coachmen are found in shoals of 3-5 individual fish that grow up to 25 cm long. They eat plankton and are found in lagoons and reefs. Juveniles will sometimes act as cleaners, removing parasites from other fish. They closely resemble Moorish idols.

SCORPIONFISH (Plate 7)

28 scorpion and lionfish occur in Seychelles. These are all either extremely well camouflaged or very flamboyant species.

Wispy waspfish *Paracentropogon longispinnis* (4)
Waspfish can grow up to 13cm. long and have depth range of 0-20m. They are sometimes seen to change colour from red to brown when in captivity. In the wild their colour makes them hard to spot among coral heads. They are found inshore, usually on reefs, on and around coral and hard areas of seabed. They eat crabs, shrimps, other waspfish, worms and jellyfish.

Scorpionfish can be divided into 3 groups. They are: lionfish, scorpionfish and stonefish.

Lionfish or firefish can grow up to 35 cm long and have highly poisonous fin spines that can cause fatalities. They include the **broad-barred firefish** *Pterois antennata* (2), **devil firesfish** *P. miles* (1) and **radial firefish** *P. radiata* (3)
They rest under rocks and in corals during the day, mostly in crevices but can be seen in the resting in the open or swimming slowly. Scorpionfish include the **hump-back scorpionfish** *Scorpaenopsis gibbosa* (6).

Scorpionfish can grow up to 21cm. long, and have fin spines which are not as poisonous as those of scorpionfish, but still very painful. These fish hunt by camouflaging themselves between the rocks on the seabed and ambushing small fish. They do not hide but as they have remarkable camouflage they are usually overlooked. The only species of **stonefish** is *Synancea verrucosa* (5). Stonefish can grow up to 40 cm long and have fin spines that contain an extremely deadly poison. Stonefish are the most venomous fish in the world and as they rest in the open care must be taken on reef flats and coral rubble. They hunt in much the same way as scorpionfish.

Plate 7

SWEETLIPS AND GATERINS (Plate 8)
The common sweetlips and gaterins found in Seychelles are:

Painted sweetlips *Diagramma pictum* (1)
Two-striped sweetlips *Plectorhynchus albovittatus* (2)
Oriental sweetlips *Plectorhynchus orientalis* (3)

These are important food fish. They are found in shallow coastal waters and reefs where they feed on benthic invertebrates, small fish, large crustaceans and molluscs. Juveniles are found in sheltered areas. they are found singly or in large groups.

MOONIES (Plate 8)

Silver moony *Monodactylus argenteus* (4)
Moonys can grow up to 27 cm long and are found in large shoals over shallow sandy coastal areas. They are also often seen in estuaries. Juveniles are solitary, but sometimes form small shoals in lagoons, estuaries and harbours. They eat detritus and plankton.

BATFISH (Plate 8)

Orbicular batfish *Platax orbicularis* (5)
The batfish can grow up to 50 cm long and has a depth range of 0-30m. Juveniles are found in estuaries and shallow lagoons. They are very common and adults are seen everywhere in small groups of 5-10 fish. They may come very close to investigate divers and snorkellers. They eat algae and invertebrates. A second species, the dusky batfish *P. pinnatus* also occurs in Seychelles.

Plate 8

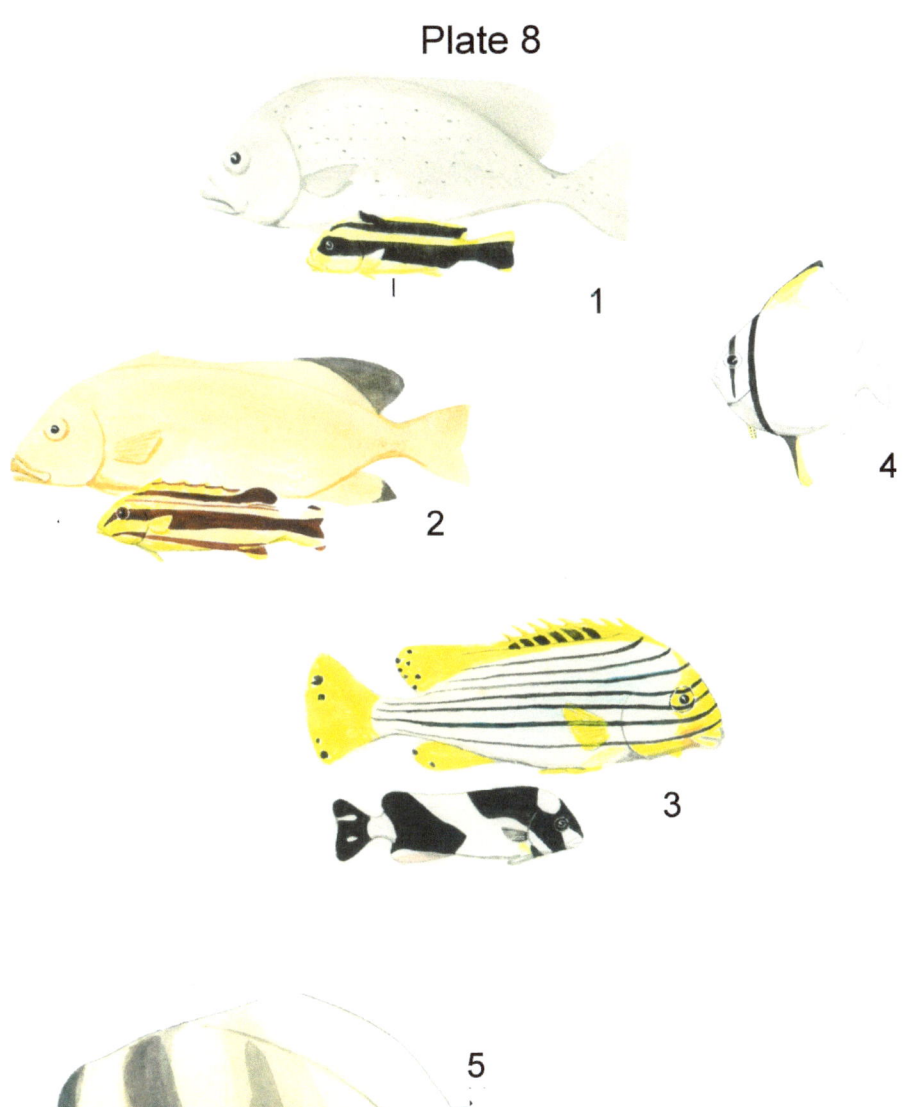

GOBIES AND BLENNIES (Plate 9)

Gobies and blennies can grow up to 10 cm long and have a depth range of 0-20 m. They are found on the bottom in sandy areas. They eat algae and plankton. There are many species and they are diverse and difficult to identify. The most distinctive blennies are the **blue-dashed rockskippers** *Bleniella periopthalmus* (3) which live on coastal rocks, grazing algae off the rocks exposed to the air. They are dashed by waves and cling on to the surface using their modified pectoral fins. The most distinctive goby species is the **fire goby** *Nemaleotris magnifica* (1). Fire gobies grow up to 9 cm long and have a depth range of 6-70 m. They are almost always seen in pairs hovering just above the bottom, facing the current to feed on zooplankton and copepods. Each individual goby will have a personal burrow which it will retreat into when frightened. Juveniles may share holes. They have a habit of flicking their long, pennant-like dorsal fins from side to side.

SAND SMELT (Plate 9)
Black-tailed sand smelt *Parapercis hexopthalma* (2)
The sand smelt is found in protected reefs and sand or rubble bottoms of shallow lagoons. It is often seen in harem groups dominated by one territorial male. It eats worms and shrimps and can grow up to 12 cm long.

LIZARDFISH (Plate 9)
Variegated lizardfish *Synodus variegatus* (4)
The colour of lizardfish changes with age. They may have a dark red band on their flanks. They are seen in deep lagoons and reefs at depths of up to 40 m. They are sometimes seen on sandy bottoms, but prefer hard substrate. They are often found in pairs. They catch small fish from passing shoals

Plate 9

SPINEFOOTS (Plate 10)
Spinefoots can grow up to 40 cm long. The fin spines are pungent and mildly poisonous. There are 6 species found in Seychelles including:

Blue-spotted spinefoot *Siganus corallinus* (1)
Shoemaker spinefoot *S. sutor* (3) and
Streamlined spinefoot *S. argenteus* (2)

They are found in shoals of 2-200 individuals swimming fast, well above the bottom, occasionally diving down to the bottom to feed. Juveniles eat algae and adults will also take small benthic invertebrates. They are important food fish in Seychelles. Adults are found on or near reefs, and juveniles in huge shoals several km. offshore, migrating to the reef just before metamorphosis.

HALFBEAK (Plate 10)
Yellowtip halfbeak *Hemiramphus marginatus* (4)
The maximum size for any of the 8 Seychelles halfbeak species is 26 cm. They are pelagic fish that almost always swim in small groups with their backs to the surface. They eat small fish, shrimps and plankton. They are livebearers. There are also several species of freshwater halfbeak, but none of them are found in Seychelles.

FLYING FISH (Plate 10)
Flying fish *Exocoeutus volitans* (5)
11 species of flying fish are present in Seychelles. They are rarely seen clearly enough for reliable identification, *E. volitans* is one of the commonest species. Flying fish grow up to 30 cm long. They are pelagic fish that are often seen from boats, leaping out of the water and gliding for up to 100 m when being chased by predators such as swordfish and tuna. They eat shrimps and plankton.

SWEEPER (Plate 10)
Black-stripe sweeper *Pempheris schwenkii* (6)
Sweepers can grow up to 20 cm long and have a depth range of 1-36 m. They form large shoals in caves and under coral heads by day, and hunt small fish, benthic and planktonic crustaceans and small invertebrates by night. They are found in shallow, clear reefs and lagoons.

GOLDIES AND CARDINALS (Plate 10)
GOLDIES
27 species of goldie are found in Seychelles. The **Sea goldie** *Anthias squamipinnis* (7) is the most common species in Seychelles, and the only easily one found in the granitic islands. Goldies can grow up to 15 cm long and are found over coral reefs at depths of

Plate 10

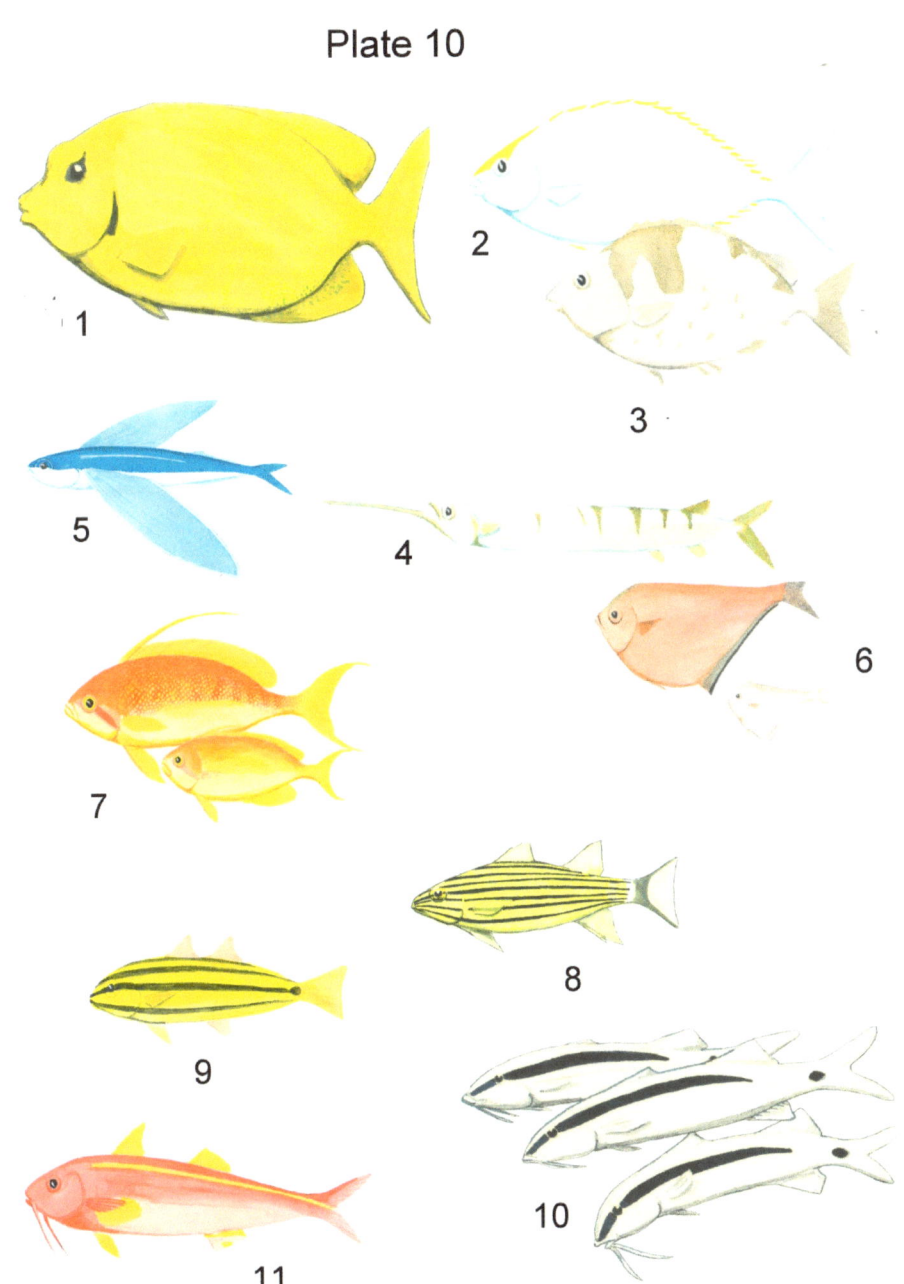

up to 55 m. They form huge shoals of one highly territorial male and several females. They are sex-changing fish, starting life female, and turning male as they grow bigger. They are eaten by several species of grouper. Colours may vary greatly according to age and sex. They eat plankton.

CARDINALS
Cardinals are a diverse family of 43 attractive species. Cardinals can grow up to 18 cm long. Two of the commonest species found in Seychelles:
Tiger cardinal *Cheilodipterus arabicus* (8)
Broadstriped cardinal *Apogon angustatus* (9).
They are found in small groups in coral caves, seaweed beds and between the spines of *Diadema* urchins on reefs. They feed on small crustaceans. Cardinals are a very common and widespread family of fish. They are found at depths of up to 40 m.

GOATFISH (Plate 10)
19 species of goatfish are found in Seychelles. Two of the most common are: The **dash-dot goatfish** *Parupeneus barberinus* (10) and **cinnabar goatfish** *Parupeneus heptacanthus* (11). They can grow up to 60 cm long and have been seen at depths of up to 100 m below the surface. They are seen on sandy and rubbly areas of substrate, and sometimes on reef flats. They eat crabs, molluscs, shrimps and small eels. Adults are solitary and juveniles are found in small groups.

ANGELFISH (Plate 11)
The common angelfish found in Seychelles are:

Two-spine angelfish *Centropyge bispinosus* (4), which grows up to 10cm. long.
Emperor angelfish *Pomacanthus imperator* (2) 40 cm.
Queen angelfish *Pomacanthus semicirculatus* (1) 40 cm. and
Royal angelfish *Pygoliptes diacanthus* (3)

Centropyge can be colourful or brown. Juvenile Emperors may be seen cleaning larger fish such as sunfish. All these species are common all over reefs. *Centropyge* will occasionally eat algae, but usually eats sponges like the other three. They are always seen singly, usually between coral heads and crevices, emerging to investigate divers and snorkellers.

Plate 11

SOLDIERFISH AND SQUIRRELFISH (Plate 12)

The common size for squirrelfish is between 15 and 30 cm, but sometimes they grow up to 35 cm. They eat plankton and shrimps, and some larger species will eat crabs and small fish. There are 27 species of soldierfish and squirrelfish found in Seychelles, but he most common are:

Seychelles soldierfish *Myripristis seychellensis* (1)
scarlet soldierfish *Myripristis pralinus* (2)
pinecone soldierfish *Myripristis murdjan* (3)
violet squirrelfish *Sargocentron violaceum* (4)
sabre squirrelfish *Sargocentron spiniferum* (5)
yellow tipped squirrelfish *Sargocentron seychellensis* (6)

Some species have venomous preopercle spines. About half of those shown are nocturnal and can be found hiding under ledges in lagoons and near the edges of reefs.

BULLSEYES (Plate 12)

Bullseyes are medium-sized, nocturnal fish usually found under overhanigs in the company of soldierfish. There are several similar species in Seychelles, including the **Moontail bullseye** *Priacanthus hamar* (7).

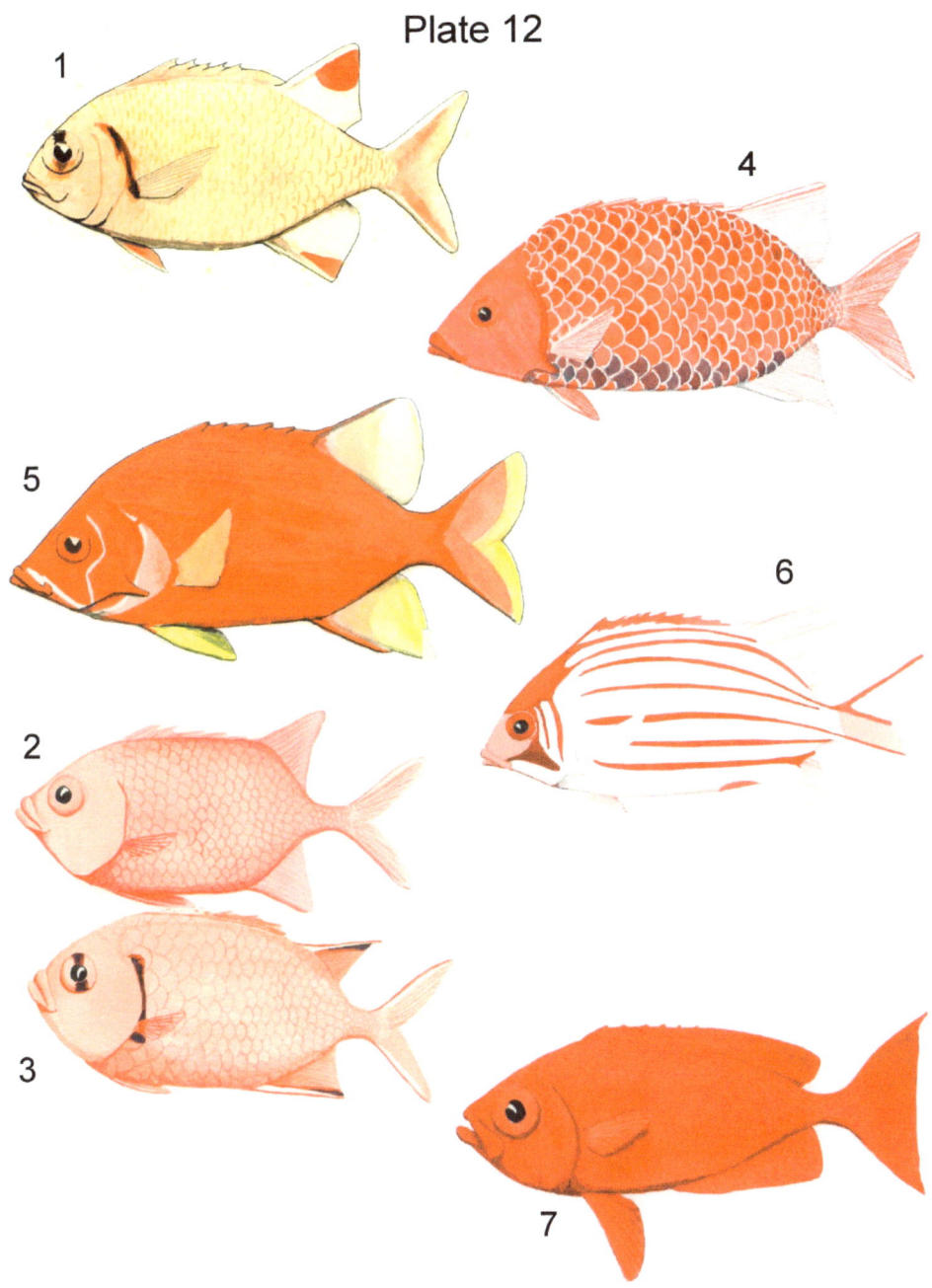

WRASSE (Plate 13)

Wrasse can grow up to 60 cm long and are found in coral, rubble and seagrass beds at depths of up to 60 cm they eat benthic invertebrates. There are 76 Seychelles species. The species commonly found are:

Spotted wrasse *Anampses meleagrides* (1)
Queen coris *Coris formosa* (2)
Rockmover wrasse *Novaculichthys teniourus* (3)
Slingjaw wrasse *Epibulus insidiator* (4)
Broomtail wrasse *Cheilinus lunulatus* (5)
Bird wrasse *Gomphosus caeruleus* (6)
Dusky wrasse *Halichoeres marginatus* (7)
Goldbar wrasse *Thalassoma hebraicum* (8)
Cleaner wrasse *Labroides dimidatus* (9)

They are solitary or occur in pairs, but are quite common. *Coris* will eat molluscs, crustaceans and sea urchins. *Epibulus* can extend their lower jaws a long way, hence the name of "slingjaw wrasse". They use the jaw as a sucking tube, extending it into crevices and sucking nekton and crustaceans out. The cleaner wrasse removes parasites from other fish which visit 'cleaner stations' for this purpose. Many species have juveniles that hide in weed and are remarkably well camouflaged.

TANG (Plate 14)

Tang can grow up to 60 cm long and are commonly found in reefs at depths of up to 90 m. The most common of the 38 Seychelles species are:

Powder blue surgeon *Acanthurus leucosternon* (6)
Bluestripe tang *A. lineatus* (2)
Convict tang *A. triostegus* (7)
Epaulette surgeonfish *A. nigricauda* (5)
Blue tang *Paracanthurus hepatus* (3)
Sailfin tang *Zebrasoma desjardinii* (1)
Bluespine unicornfish *Naso unicornis* (8)
Orangespine unicornfish *Naso elegans* (4)

Eagle rays are often seen eating the eggs of *A. nigricauda* immediately after a spawning. They are seen singly, sometimes in shoals. They eat long filaments of algae attached to rocks. Male *A. lineatus* have venomous caudal spines and use these to control feeding territory for their large harems of females.

Plate 14

PARROTFISH (Plate 15)

Parrotfish are among the commonest reef fish, there are 26 species in Seychelles. As many species are variable, with sexual dimorphism and sex change they can be extremely difficult to identify. The common parrotfish in Seychelles are:

Ember parrotfish *S. rubroviolaceus* (1) 70 cm
Daisy parrotfish *Chlorurus sordidus* (2) 40 cm
Marbled parrotfish *Leptoscarus vaigiensis* (3) 35 cm and
Red-barred parrotfish *S. caudofasciatus* (4) 50 cm
Blue-barred parrotfish *Scarus ghobban* (5) 90 cm_
Green humphead parrotfish *Bolbometopon muricatum* (6)130cm

All species eat algae and coral. Parrotfish are some of the most common reef fish in Seychelles, and are often seen in large shoals, grazing on algae and coral. Parrotfish are an important food fish. All species change sex from female to male except for *Leptoscarus* which is also one of the only genera of parrotfish where males have small teeth on the upper jaw.

TRIGGERS AND FILEFISH (Plate 16)
The most common triggerfish in Seychelles are:

Honeycomb trigger *Cantherhines pardalis* (3)
Picasso trigger *Rhinecanthus aculeatus* (2)
Titan trigger *Balistoides virescens* (3)

The only filefish that has been seen is:

Harlequin filefish *Oxymonacnthus longirostris* (1)

Picasso triggers sleep on their sides and make a whining noise when disturbed. They eat small echinoderms, fish, crustaceans and benthic invertebrates. Harlequin filefish exclusively eat acropora, and so were heavily affected by the coral bleaching. They can be found in small groups in *Acropora* corals. One species, the blacksaddle puffer *Canthigaster bennetti* is a mimic of Valentini's sharpnose puffer *Canthigaster valentini* and is treated in the puffer fish section even though it is really a filefish.

Plate 16

PUFFERS, PORCUPINE FISH AND BOXFISH (Plate 17)

The most common species of puffer in Seychelles are:

Valentini's sharpnose puffer *Canthigaster valentini* (6) 11 cm.
Pearl toby *C. margaritata* (10) 30 cm.
Starry puffer *Arothron stellatus* (8) 120 cm.
Black spotted puffer *A. nigropunctatus* (7) 33 cm and
Blacksaddle puffer *Paraluteres prionurus* (5) 11 cm.

The commonest porcupine fish is:

Spotfin porcupinefish *D. hystrix* (9) 91 cm.

The only species of cowfish found in Seychelles is:

Longhorn cowfish *Lactoria cornuta* (1) 46 cm.

The common boxfish are:

Shortnose boxfish *Ostracion nasus* (4) 30 cm.
Whitespotted boxfish *O. meleagris* (2) 25 cm.
Golden boxfish *O. cubicus* (3) 45 cm.

The **blacksaddle puffer** is a mimic of **Valentini's sharpnose puffer** and the two species are often found in mixed shoals. Puffers eat algae and molluscs. They are found over coral and rubble. They are territorial shoaling fish. Porcupine fish are nocturnal and can be found under table corals and in caves during the day, coming out to graze on crustaceans and molluscs at night. They are solitary fish. The cowfish is found in sandy areas. Adults are solitary, but juveniles form small shoals. In some countries they are often dried and used as ornaments. They blow sand away from the bottom to get at benthic invertebrates. Boxfish eat sponges and algae. Females are always seen very close to males.

Plate 17

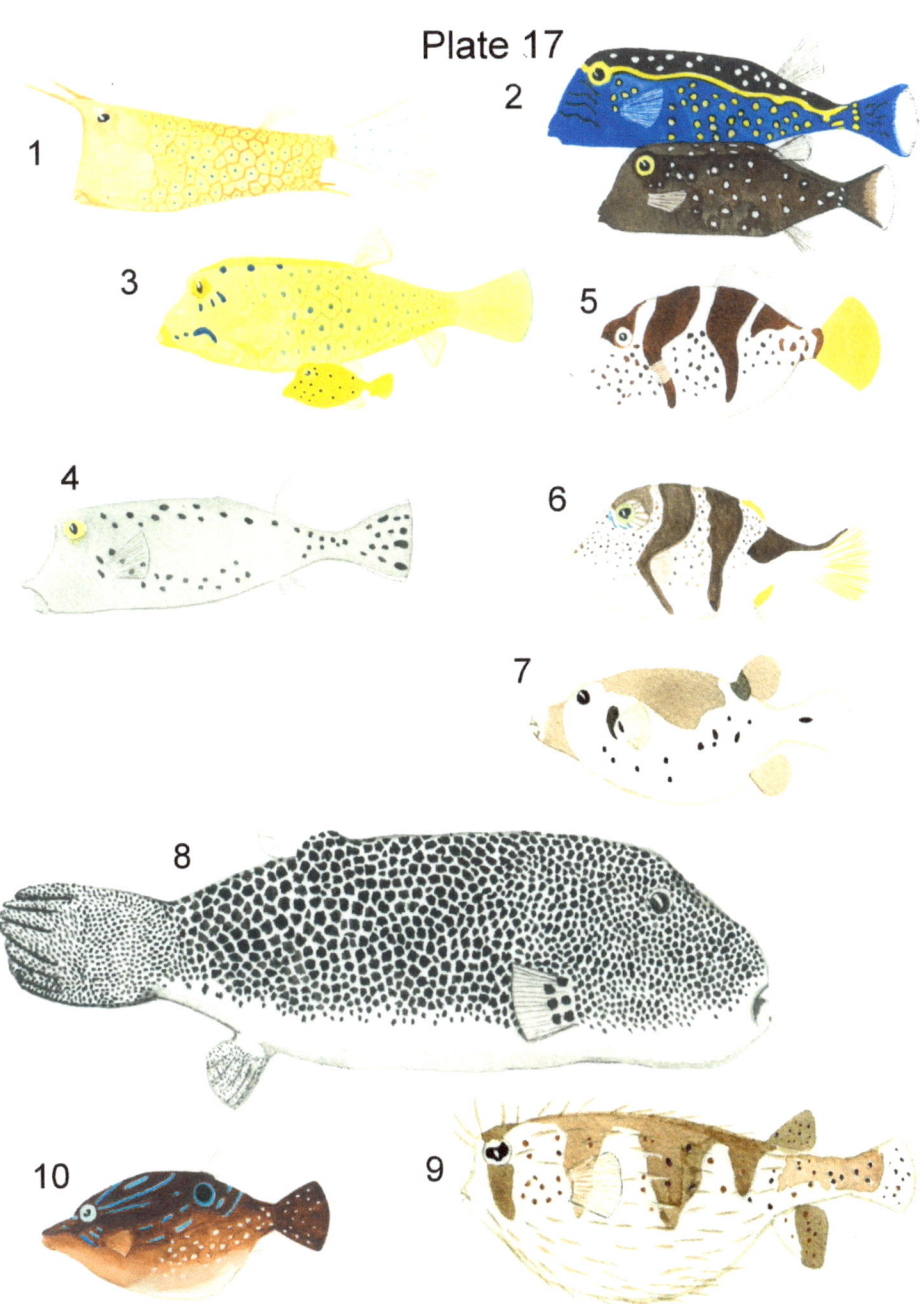

SNAPPERS AND EMPERORS (Plate 18)

Snappers are reef fish, and found in large shoals around coral formations, caves and shipwrecks during the day. The juveniles inhabit seagrass beds. They eat crustaceans, small fish and cephalopods. There are 17 species of snapper, but the ones that are most commonly seen are:

common bluestripe snapper *Lutjanus kasmira* (1)
humpback red snapper *Lutjanus gibbus* (2)
bigeye snapper *Lutjanus lutjanus* (3)
emperor red snapper *Lutjanus sebae* (4)
humphead snapper *Lutjanus sanguineus* (6)
dory snapper *Lutjanus fulviflamma* (5)
thumbprint emperor *Lethrinus harak* (7)

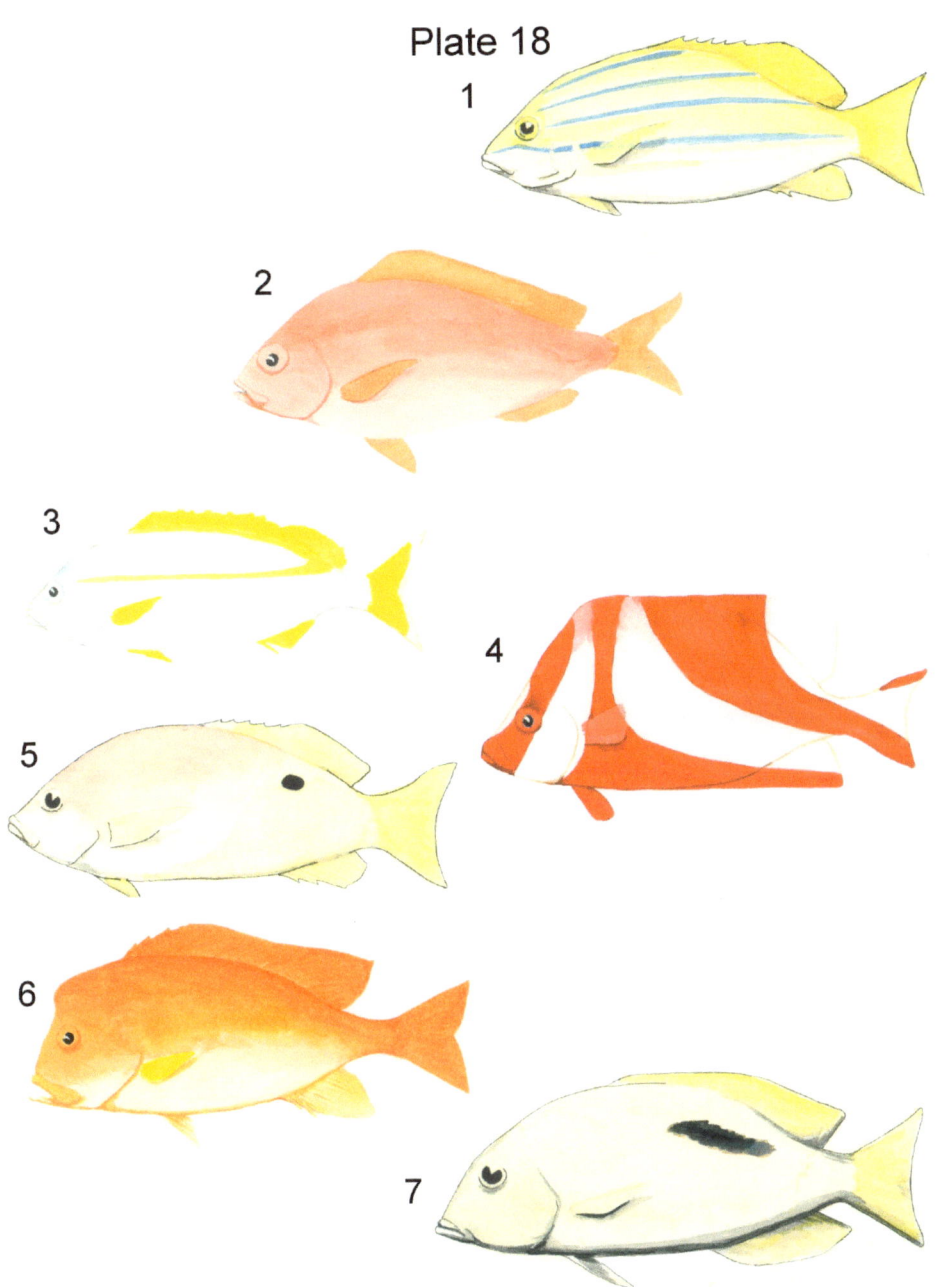

GAMEFISH (Plate 19)

Dorado *Coryphaena hippurus* (1)
The dorado (of which there are two species) is one of the most commonly caught gamefish in Seychelles. It is found mainly in open water, at depths of 0-85 m, but is sometimes seen in coastal areas. It is a highly migratory species. They can grow up to 2 m long and weigh up to 4 kg. The oldest recorded is 4 years. It eats all small fish, crustaceans and squid. It can be attracted in large numbers to stationary floating objects such as boats.

King mackerel *Scomberomorus* sp. (2)
King mackerel or kingfish can grow to over 1 m long and can weigh up to 12.5 kg. They have a depth range of 50-200 m. They are found in large shoals. They eat small fish, squid and mantis shrimps.

Swordfish *Xiphias gladius* (3)
Swordfish are unusual in that they are scaleless and lack pelvic fins. They can grow up to 4 ½ m. long and weigh up to 500 kg. It eats fish and squid. Juveniles have small spiny scales similar to those of marlin. They hatch with a fully developed sword.. In adults, the length of the sword is about 1/3 of the body length. Swordfish are found in open water.

Sailfish *Istiophorus platypterus* (4)
Sailfish can grow up to 3.5 m long and can weigh up to 100 kg. They can live for up to 13 years. They are found in open water at depths of up to 200 m. Like marlin, they change colour when excited. They eat fish, squid and crustaceans.

Marlin
Marlin are very similar to swordfish in appearance, but are slightly shorter, only growing up to 4 ½ m long. They have a depth range of 0-915 m, and can weigh up to 750 kg. They have small spiny scales. There are 3 species found in Seychelles:
Black marlin *Makaira indica* (6), **Indo-Pacific blue marlin** *Makaira mazara* and **striped marlin** *Tetrapturus audax* (5).

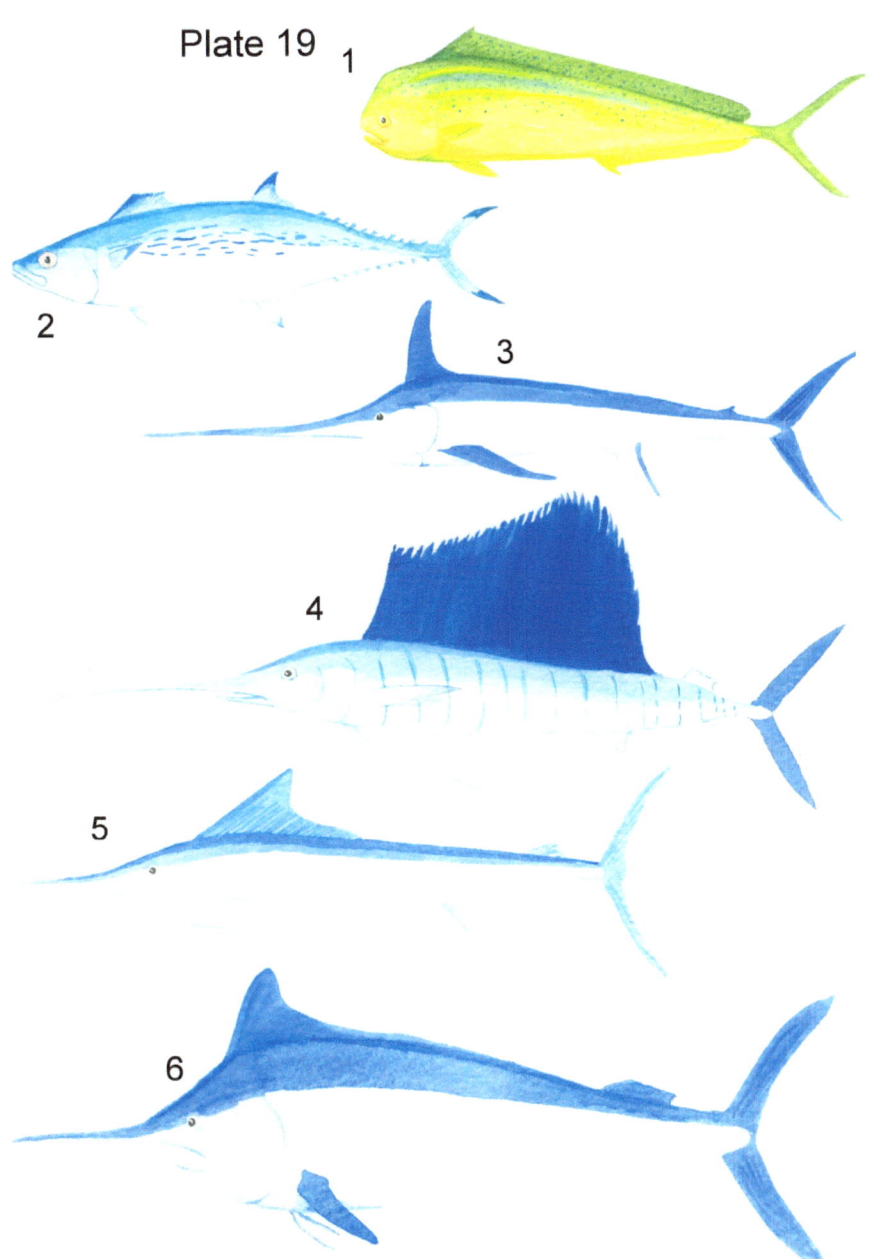

Plate 19

JACK (Plate 20)

The standard size for a jack is between 40cm and 1m. They are widely used s an important food fish. They are found in medium sized shoals, usually over rocky or coral areas, but some species will more commonly be seen over sandy areas. They eat small invertebrates and fish. There are 12 species of *Carangoides* and 2 species of *Trachinotus*. Most are similar in appearance and the **snubnose jack** *Trachinotus blochii* (1) is typical. The maximum weight of any of these species is 3.4 kg.

TUNA (Plate 20)

Tuna can grow up to 2 m long and have a depth range of 0-300 m they are seen in open water near the surface. They eat fish. The common tuna in Seychelles are:
Bonito *Euthynnus affinnis* (4)
Albacore *Thynnus albacore* (5)
Skipjack tuna *Katsuwonus pelamis* (3) and
Rainbow runner *Elegatis bipinnulata* (2)
They are very major food fish. They release eggs in huge numbers with many intervals and are strongly migratory.

Plate 20

DAMSELFISH (Plate 21-22)
The 55 Seychelles damsels can be divided into 3 groups, the clownfish, the territorial damsels and the shoaling damsels.

The clownfish are the **skunk clownfish** *Amphiprion akallopisos* (21.7), that grows up to 11 cm long and the **Seychelles clownfish** *A. fuscocaudatus* (21.6), 14 cm. The skunk clownfish is only found in the anemone *Heteractis magnifica*, but the Seychelles clownfish has been seen in many. Each anemone can contain 1 large female, 1 small functioning male and several stunted juveniles. When the female is removed, the male undergoes a sexchange and the largest juvenile becomes a functioning male.

The shoaling damsels include the **sergeant major** *Abudefduf saxatillis* (21.1) 22 cm, **scissortail sergeant major** *A. sexfasciatus* (21.2) 16cm, **white-tail dascyllus** *Dascyllus aruanus* (21.5) 10 cm, **domino** *D. trimaculatus* (21.3) 11 cm and **reticulated dascyllus** *D. reticulatus* (21.4) 9 cm. Sergeant majors are very common and will come extremely close to divers and snorkellers. Sergeant majors eat algae, invertebrate larvae, crustaceans and small fish. Juveniles clean turtles. *Dascyllus* inhabit *Acropora* corals, and are seen all over reefs. Juvenile dominos often inhabit sea anemones.

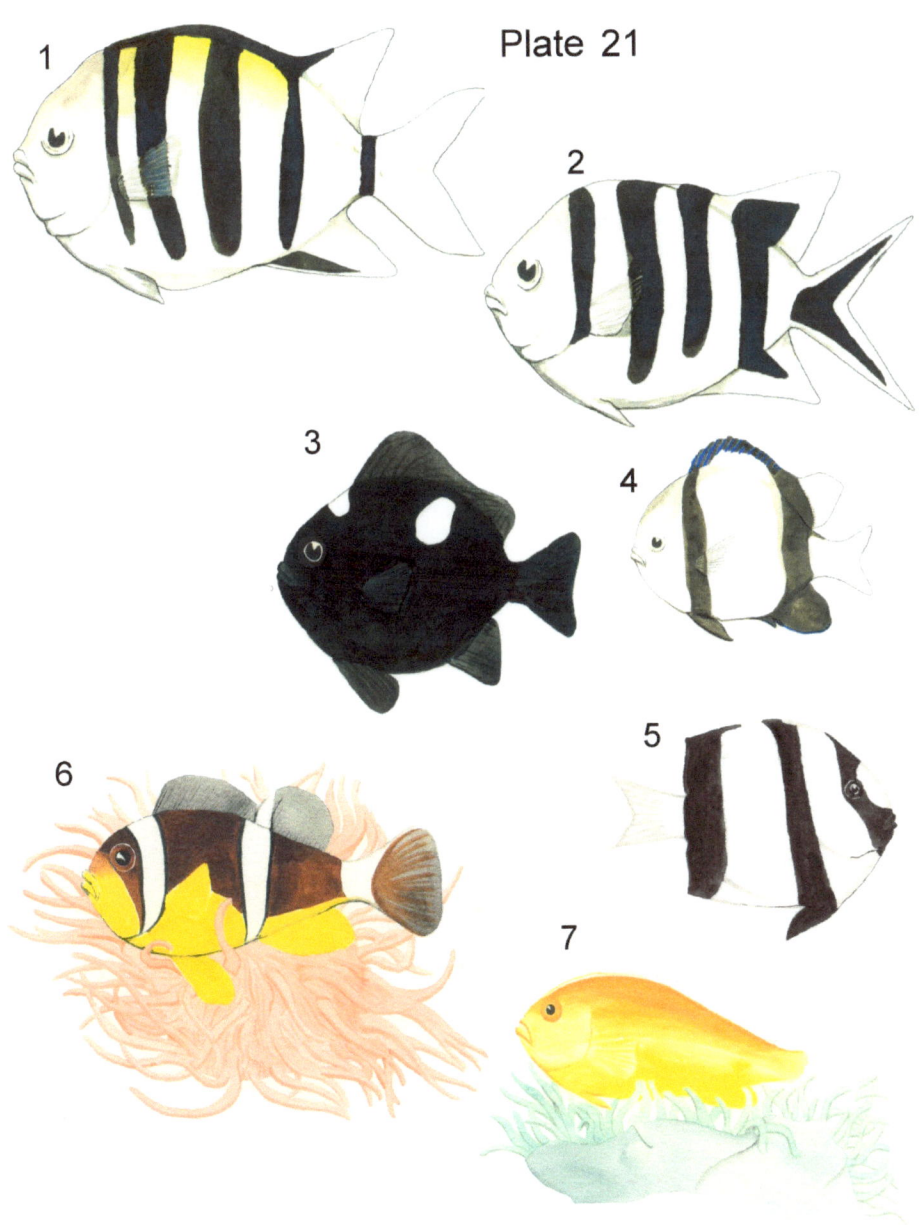

The territorial damsels are the **one-spot damsel** *Chrysiptera unimaculata* (22.5) 10 cm, **sulphur damsel** *Pomacentrus sulfureus* (22.2) 11 cm, **sapphire damsel** *P. pavo* (22.4) 10cm and the **caerulean damsel** *P. caerulaeus* (22.6) 10cm. The **three-line damsel** *P. trilineatus* (22.5) 10 cm is very similar to the **one-spot damsel** but tends to be much darker (often black with blue markings). The territories of these fish are recognisable by the growth of weed caused by the forcible expulsion of any grazer that ventures near.

Colourful shoaling damsels are the **chocolate dip damsel** *Chromis dimidata* (22.6) 9 cm and the **blue chromis** *C. caerulea* (22.3) 6.5 cm. *Chromis* inhabit flat rubbly areas near reefs.

GROUPERS (Plate 23)

The common size for a grouper is somewhere between 60 cm and 1 m, and the depth range is 1-65 m. Groupers are a common food fish that, in Seychelles, are mainly caught on handlines. Juveniles are usually found in shallow reefs and adults in deep ones, where they hide in caves by day. They are mainly nocturnal. 36 species occur in Seychelles; the most commonly seen species are:

black-saddled grouper *Plectropomus laevis* (1)
peacock hind *Cephalopholis argus* (2)
white-spotted grouper *Epinephelus caruleopunctatus* (3)
potato cod *Epinephelus tukula* (4)
blacktip grouper *E. fasciatus* (5)
sixline soapfish *Grammistes sexlineatus* (6)
Yellow-edged lyretail *Variola louti* (7)

HAWKFISH (Plate 23)
Blackside hawkfish *Paracirrhites forsteri* (1)
The blackside hawkfish is one of 9 species recorded in Seychelles. It grows up to 22cm long and can be found at depths of up to 35 m below the surface. The colour changes with age and the head can be black, grey, brown or white, but except for when the whole head is black, there are always black spots around the nose. The black stripe may be red at the front, plain black or dark brown. The whole body can be brown, red with black around the tail or dark brown with a yellow tail. There is usually a pale coloured stripe on either side of the black band. It tends to perch on the outermost branches of *acropora* and is a territorial species and a minor food fish. It eats small fish, crustaceans and isopods.

Plate 23

ESTUARINE AND FRESHWATER FISH (Plate 24)

Golden panchax *Pachypanchax playfairii* (1)
Golden panchax can grow up to 10 cm long. They produce 50-200 eggs at a time, which are laid in weed or in sand. They eat worms, small fish and mosquitoes. This is a common species in freshwater aquaria.

Tilapia *Oreochromis mossambicus* (2)
The tilapia can grow up to 40 cm long and can weigh over 1 kg. The maximum reported age is 11 years. They eat plants, detritus and plankton. Although this is the commonest freshwater fish in Seychelles it was only introduced in the mid 20th century. They are used as food fish in some areas of Africa, but not in Seychelles.

Mud gudgeon *Ophiocara porocephala* (3)
Mud gudgeons can grow up to 34 cm long. They are found in estuaries, river mouths and brackish creeks where they sit on the bed and are often overlooked due to their good camouflage. They eat detritus, nekton and shrimps, which they hunt by hiding under rocks and ambushing their prey.

Mudskippers (3)
There are two species of mudskipper found in Seychelles and they are *Periopthalmus kalolo* and *P. argentlineatus*. *P. kalolo* can grow up to 14 cm long and *P. argentlineatus* up to 19 cm. They are extremely common and amphibious, being commonly seen on mud banks, mangrove roots and stones with their tails dipped in the water. They can stay out of the water for up to 37 hours if kept moist. They eat worms, insects and crustaceans.

Plate 24

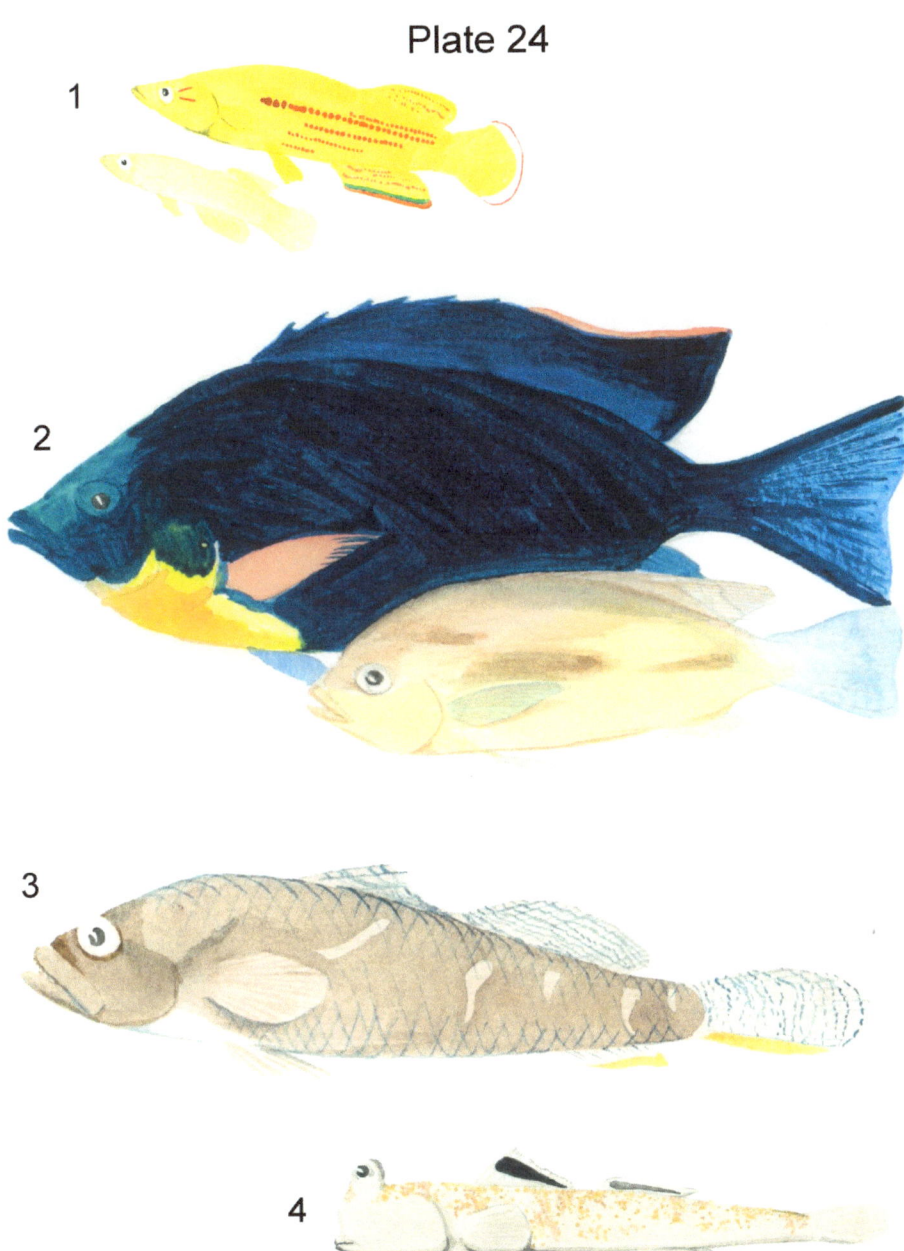

www.ingramcontent.com/pod-product-compliance
Ingram Content Group UK Ltd.
Pitfield, Milton Keynes, MK11 3LW, UK
UKHW061140180426
11947UKWH00004B/17